THE ANGEL OF THE POINTING HAND

The
Brotherhood
of
Angels and Men

The Brotherhood
of
Angels and Men

By GEOFFREY HODSON

With a foreword by Annie Besant

*This publication made possible
with the assistance of the Kern Foundation*

The Theosophical Publishing House
Wheaton, Ill. U.S.A.
Madras, India/London, England

First Quest edition 1982. No part of this book
may be reproduced in any manner without
written permission except for quotations embodied in critical
articles or reviews. For additional information
write to: The Theosophical Publishing House,
306 West Geneva Road,
Wheaton, Illinois 60187.
This is a publication of the Theosophical Publishing House,
a department of the Theosophical Society in America.

Library of Congress Cataloging in Publication Data
Hodson, Geoffrey
  Brotherhood of angels and men.

  Reprint. Originally published: London:
Theosophical Publishing House, 1927.   (Brotherhood
of angels and of men series)
  1. Theosophy.   I. Title.   II. Series: Hodson,
Geoffrey. Brotherhood of angels and of men series
(Wheaton, Ill.)
BP565.H63B76   1982   229'.934   81-53012
ISBN 0-8356-0559-0 (pbk.)   AACR2

Printed in the United States of America

CONTENTS

FOREWORD

I HAVE been asked to introduce this book to a sceptical world, and yet a world in which every religion, each scripture, asserts the fact of the existence of Angels and of their occasional appearances among men. They may be called by any name —angels, nature-spirits, devas (shining ones), elementals. Angels or devas is the term often applied to the higher grades, nature spirits, elementals, fairies, to the lower.

At this period of evolution, we are under the influence of a natural force, which will slowly become predominant in every department of nature; it is the force which works for co-operation between angelhood and humanity and seeks to build bridges by which the two great races, human and angelic, may combine for their mutual good. These bridges are ceremonies, chiefly in religions and in Freemasonry, for these deal with the highest spiritual worlds through all worlds, the superhuman, the human, down to the lowest, the sub-human.

I have not studied the subject closely, as Mr. Geoffrey Hodson has done, but his observations are congruous with the many details in Hindu books and with my general knowledge on the subject, gained in travelling in different countries as well as by reading. In Hungary, for instance, the nature spirits of the earth seemed specially active, quaint little creatures, veritable gnomes, entirely different from the gorgeous hosts of Kubera in India, though both are concerned with the mineral kingdom.

This book is specially interesting in the suggestions made by the angels of ways of reaching them, and as to mutual co-operation, and many may be inclined to work for "The Brotherhood of Angels and of Men."

1927   ANNIE BESANT, D.L.

PREFACE TO THE FIFTH REPRINT

A S I consider a Preface to this reprint of *The Brotherhood of Angels and of Men*, I find myself in thought and memory back again deep in the woods of the small village of Sheepscombe in Gloucestershire. There, in 1924, as I was endeavouring to observe and record descriptions of the nature-spirit life, I almost suddenly found my consciousness translated (if I may use such a term) to the level at which I beheld the great Member of the Angelic Hosts who named himself to me, "Bethelda." While I was fully conscious and able to dictate, he transmitted to me ideas which have gradually become published in five successive books.*

---

* *The Brotherhood of Angels and of Men, The Angelic Hosts, Be Ye Perfect, Man the Triune God, The Supreme Splendour.*

Whenever I return to England I always revisit the much-loved village, the cottage and the garden and the woods where my mind became opened to some knowledge of the Kingdom of the Gods. Indeed, a book of that title, illustrated by a South African artist, Miss Ethelwynne Quail, is just now re-appearing in its seventh edition.

Thus, I understand, the idea of collaboration between Angels and men in the service of God and humanity has reached large numbers in many parts of the world, and the guidance given in this book has been practised beneficially by many people.

I am grateful to the Publishers of these books and especially to Dr. Annie Besant who so generously encouraged me from the beginning and wrote a Foreword to this work.

GEOFFREY HODSON

Adyar, 1973

VISION

Formless Worlds — The Real			World of Form — The Unreal

The River of Truth

THE BRIDGE — THE ROAD

World	Angels	Rulers of Worlds	Rulers of Rulers of Worlds	Selves
World of Creative Power	Angels of Music		Rulers of Rulers of Worlds	Our Angel Selves / Our True Selves
World of Unity	Angels of Beauty and of Art			
World of Joy and Peace	Angels of Joy	Rulers of Worlds		Our Immortal Selves
World of Thought	Building Angels			Our Mortal Thinking Selves
World of Feeling	Building, Guardian and Nature Angels	Sylph / Salamander / Undine		Our Mortal Feeling Selves
World of Flesh	Building Angels	Brownie / Gnome		Our Mortal Solid Selves

The Universe as Described by the Angel in His Teaching

I

THE BROTHERHOOD

THE ideal of this brotherhood is to draw angels and men, two branches of the infinite family of God, into close co-operation. The chief purpose of such co-operation is to uplift the human race.

To this end the angels, on their side, are ready to participate as closely as possible in every department of human life and in every human activity that holds co-operation in view.

Those members of the human race who will throw open heart and mind to their brethren of the other sphere, will find an immediate response, and a gradually increasing conviction of its reality.

While the angels make no conditions, and impose no restrictions or limits to the activities and devel-

1

opments resulting from co-operation, they assume
that no human brother would invoke them for personal and material gain. They ask for the accep-
tance of the motto of the Brotherhood* and its
practical application to human life in every aspect.

They ask those who would invoke their presence,
to concentrate the whole of their faculties on the
development of the qualities of:

>Purity,
>Simplicity,
>Directness and
>Impersonality,

as well as on the acquirement of knowledge of the
great Plan whereby the spiritual, intellectual and
material constituents, composing alike man and the
universe, maintain the ordered march of evolu-
tionary progress. In this way the fundamental basis
of every human activity will be the teachings and
doctrines of that Divine and Ancient Wisdom
which has always reigned supreme as the directing
influence in the councils of the angels.

The special divisions of the angel host with
whom co-operation would be immediately practi-
cable and beneficial are:

>The Angels of Power,
>The Angels of Healing,
>The Guardian Angels of the Home,
>The Angels who build Form, ever embody-
>ing archetypal ideals,

---

* See Chap. IV.

The Angels of Nature,
The Angels of Music and
The Angels of Beauty and Art.

The Angels of Power

The Angels of Power will teach men to release the deeper levels of spiritual energy latent within them, and will fill, inform, inspire and charge every human activity with that fiery and resistless energy which is their most prominent characteristic. At present, they find in ceremonial a natural medium for their gifts and for their desire to aid their human brethren. Ceremonial always attracts their attention, and, properly performed, provides a channel through which they can pour their forces. They are present at every religious ceremony, participating according to the measure of their capacity, and to the degree which the ceremony itself permits; they can work more powerfully if the mental attitude of the officiants and participants is receptive.

The Angels of the Healing Art

The Healing Angels—under their mighty Head, the Archangel Raphael—being filled with love for their human brethren, pursue their work continuously. Their presence by the sick beds of men is a reality, though the minds and hearts of the majority of those responsible for healing of sickness are closed against them. Many who suffer and have suffered know them well. They stand in their thousands on the spiritual and mental thresholds of every sick-room, in hospital or home, eager to enter in. Hitherto, but few have succeeded, the barriers upraised by human minds are often insuperable; should they break through these in spite of opposition, the precious healing which they bear in outstretched arms would be lost, dissipated in the effort to overcome resistance.

The Guardian Angels of the Home

The Guardian Angels love the homely ways of men, they desire to share the hours of labour and of ease; they love children and their play, and all the happy atmosphere of the home. They would guard men's homes, keeping away all influences of danger and of strife, of darkness and disease. They hear the children's prayers at night and bear them to the Lord, and they vivify every human thought of love by adding something of their love and life; often they bear the thought on its mission and pour it, illumined and increased, into the receiver's heart. They tend the aged and the sick. They are ever ready to shield from harm. To all whose hearts and homes are open to them, they would gladly come, bringing many blessings from on high—blessings of harmony and love.

The Angels who Build

The Building Angels guide growth in every world, and, shaping it according to the law, seek ever to improve, to perfect and inspire. Each immortal spark which finds birth in worlds of thought, of feeling and of flesh, and, growing, becomes man, owes all its vehicles, or bodies, to the angel builders; so also do every gem, every plant, every animal, every globe, and every universe. They stand in graded orders, these builders, each labouring at his own height, the lesser ones build gems, the greater ones worlds; there are some who build the outer forms of angels and of men.

It is lack of recognition of their place and aid that has made childbirth in later times a period of agony or death. When men invoke their aid, they will teach the human race how to bring forth their kind with joy, they will see that the great sacrifice is no longer marred by fear and cries of agony and woe.

These angels who build man, have, as their Queen, a Holy One, who won freedom from the burden of the flesh and, ascending joined the Angel Hosts. She labours ever for the cause of human motherhood, and even now is bending all Her mighty strength and calling all Her Angel Court to labour for the upliftment of womanhood throughout the world. Through Her angel messengers, She Herself is present at every human birth, unseen and unknown, it is true, but if men would but open their eyes She would be revealed.

She sends this message through the Brotherhood to men:

"In the Name of Him whom long ago I bore, I come to your aid. I have taken every woman into my heart, to hold there a part of her that through it I may help her in her time of need.

"Uplift the women of your race till all are seen as queens, and to such queens let every man be as a king, that each may honour each, seeing the other's royalty. Let every home, however small, become a court, every son a knight, every child a page. Let all treat all with chivalry, honouring in each their royal parentage, their kingly birth; for there is royal blood in every man; all are the children of the KING."

The Angels of Nature

The Nature Angels are widely distributed, each dwelling and working in his own element. They range from brownie, elf and fairy sprite, through undine and sylph, to the creatures of the fire. The angels of nature are to be found everywhere around men's haunts, in tree, in flower, in stone, in cloud, ensouling every form.

The growth of crops, of fruit and flowers, is under their control. It is they who bring, when men so live as to create them, earthquake and storm and flood. If humanity would invoke their aid, they might learn from them how all the moods and products of nature may be controlled. The climate and the weather of the world answer to law; salamander, undine and sylph of storm are but the agents of that law.

The Angels of Music

If you would appeal to the gods of Music you must rise to those levels of the Self where creative energy, creative power, is stored; for the Angels of

Music are but the embodiments of the creative Word of God, the expressions of His Voice. When He speaks, a mighty burst of song springs from their hearts and pours its resonance throughout the graded order of their race.

They sing in their myriads in answer to the Word of God. Their sound is as of a million harps touched by immortal hands, their voice is like the surging of the sea. From the centre of the Universe, like a mighty tidal flood, their song goes forth in wave on wave of glory, as order after order answers to the Word; they send the chorus forth, outwards to the confines of the Universe.

Creation never ceases. His Voice is heard continually, the Voice of Him Who, seeing visions of extra universal space, of cosmic ideations, speaks, telling His vision, and telling, calls the vision forth, creating it in form within His Universe. At His Voice Angels of Music leap from His Lips to become the agents of the power of Sound; all the world of creative power is filled with the harmony of His Voice; and the Angels are to Him as harps, as glorious stringed instruments, responding to His will. As they sing, they glow with the colour of their song. They live in worlds of Light and Sound, they are the expression of cosmic hues and cosmic song within the limits of a universe.

Our Logos is a lens through which the light of myriads of universes passes into His own; He is a mighty organ-pipe under the hand of the Absolute. All the Logoi of all the universes answer to the cosmic keyboard on which It plays. Thus Colour and Sound are born, those wondrous twins, and brought within the limitations of earthly time and space.

Every angel, and every man in his true self, glows with that wondrous light, answers to the Divine Song, knows well the tones of the Creative Voice. The true Self in man is lens and organ-pipe in miniature; as he sings and glows in answer to the Voice of God he reproduces in his grade but with exactitude, every tone and microtone of his Voice, every shade of the spectrum of His light. The splendours of that rainbow-hued world pass downwards to the lesser self, and there hover, that even the lowest self may hear.

The mission of the Music angels is to bear this radiance of a million prisms, this surging of a million planets, downwards to the ears of men, outwards into material worlds, that even tree and plant and mole beneath the earth may hear the Voice of God and, hearing it, obey. Every sound you hear on earth is an echo of His Voice, and every light in every colour comes from the dazzling radiance of His Eyes.

You cannot call these angels down into the lowest self; to see and hear them you must rise towards their world; as you cross its threshold you will see the mighty throng, ever bathed in myriad rainbow hues, ever chanting forth in anthem-tones the Words of God. Through the sound of their trumpets and flutes, the beating of their wings, and through the light of the fiery splendour of their eyes and the radiant beauty of their forms comes the music of their voices. Ever they sing thus and play from birth to death of universes—they remain the choral orchestra of God.

They are in need of human ears and human hearts, that through them they may bring our world in tune, that men may answer ever more and more to the sound and rhythm of their song. To them, all men and all angels are instruments, every faculty of mind and heart is a string. They watch each new-born race with eagerness, seeing in it the promise of new instruments, a wider range of tone, another organ-pipe to answer to the breath of God. They see the unity of all, know each as part of the one great instrument upon which God plays that which He hears beyond the realms of time and space. Through this instrument—through all the manifold music—throbs the beating of His Heart, the rhythm of the universal pulse. All the movements of the stars, the lighting and setting of suns, the birth of planets and their death, the evolution of the race, the waves that break upon the shore, the rise and fall of continents, the melting of the Polar seas, the beating of the hearts of men, the germination of the seed, all these respond to the rhythm of the pulsing heart of God.

This is the burden of the song the Gods of Music sing.

The Angels of Beauty and of Art

Everything divine is beautiful, expressing in its degree the perfect beauty of the Absolute.

The greater the density in which God limits Himself, the deeper His beauty lies hidden. Some among the Angel hosts, seeing the beauty of their God, themselves embody it, and take it as their duty in the world of form to aid the builders of forms, that they may fashion all things, never forgetting the beauty of the pattern by which they work.

These Angels of Beauty seek to mould both growing and completed forms, that more and more the hidden loveliness may shine forth. As Music angels are the voice of God, these angels are His Hand, with which He paints upon the canvas of the universe the picture of the vision He has seen.

Every time a man aspires towards the Beautiful, and tries to model, paint or draw according to the highest he can see, he makes himself akin to the angels of the Hand of God; for a time their rhythm becomes his. If he called them they would come and add their vision to his own, their genius of colour and of form, would wake in him their thirst for all things beautiful, would strive to stimulate his mind to break the conventions and the limitations of his time. They would implant new theories, fresh ideals within his brain; so that the tendency of human mind to set a limit and fix a law would be overcome, and creative genius, hid deep as though within a prison, would be released. So his soul would be set free, and mounting on the wings of art might attain the vision that is ever new, might override the canons of the past; for even the Beauty of God is subject to the law of change, and grows in splendour day by day.

The Angels of Colour and of Form would bring to man this growing beauty, this ever-increasing wonder, this infinite loveliness of God, that every man might share with them the honour which is theirs of acting as the Hand of the Supreme Artist. Invoke angels in your schools of art, invite them to your aid; then ugliness shall be banished and all the world be more beautiful.

Their message to men is that Beauty ranks high among the offerings on the altar of the Gods, that Beauty should be regarded as a virtue, and ugliness be branded as a sin; that every child from birth should see only what is lovely, graceful and delicate.

Beauty is not born, nor can it die, it is eternal. Only a fragment of Beauty's self can become manifest, only a gleam from the eternal Sun of Beauty can shine through a universe; men seeing it, and dazzled by the sight, think that they see the whole, though the whole can never be seen by angel or by man. But the fragment grows, the radiance of the gleam increases, as more and more the universe embodies it. More and more the Self and Beauty appear as one in manifested worlds, as they are one in worlds unmanifest.

True beauty is ever new; and this is the sign by which you may distinguish between the false and the true. False beauty, product of the lesser selves, changes not, is fixed, and like all things that are "fixed" in a universe which is ever growing, is old from the moment it is born.

As there is a motion throughout the universe, so

motion must be suggested by true beauty. There is no beauty in a picture of death, though death itself is not without beauty. Beauty is the soul of all natural things, and lies hid in every virtue, especially love. You need no other standard, require no other law; nor is there any other virtue so great as the love of the beautiful, for beauty is the essence of them all.

Every law you frame, and every statute you enact, should be tested by this question: "Will the result be beautiful?" This is the ideal by which a citizen should measure his conduct and his duty to the State. This is the standard for the nations in their Councils and their Leagues, for with one glance the artist Ruler of a world can estimate the worth of governments and kings. To Him, the measure of a nation's ugliness is the measure of its mismanagement of affairs; the measure of a nation's beauty, as of the true royalty of its king, is that of the progress it has made. Welcome, then, as continents, as nations, as men, the presence of the angels of the Hand of God, the Devas of Beauty, for they will fill your worlds of feeling and of thought with such an impress of their gift that your more solid selves will be unable to resist. Aided by the angels of the Hand of God, all men may become artists, for the Vision Splendid will come so close that even the dullest eyes must see. Poets, dreamers, painters, sculptors, will arise in every family, till all the world becomes a studio, and earth and stone and brick are recognised as clay for the modeller's hand.

You shall build cities fairer than were ever seen in Greece, for you are Greece reincarnate; but you have grown since then; the angels who taught in Greece have grown since then. Together we might fill whole continents with cities fairer than those of old.

You shall mould your thoughts, your feelings and your flesh; you shall build a Race godlike in its beauty and its strength; the angel hosts will come to aid you in your task.

This is the vision of the future that we bring, a future of limitless possibilities of splendour, when once more the children of God, angels and men, come together for the fulfilment of the Plan. Following are messages I have received directly from the Angelic Kingdom.

II
THE FIRST MESSAGE

SINCE the Great One has drawn so close to our world and to yours, it is of first importance that the bridge between the two should be fashioned, that the time may be hastened when it may be used freely from either side. We must devise better means of communication; and your studies might well have for their object the widening of the bridge and the instruction of your brethren in its use. They will find us coming more than half-way to meet them, for the Lord Himself has decreed that we should draw together in closer bonds of unity.

The first essential on your side is a belief in our existence; to that end, more information about us must be given, and presented in such a manner that

14

it will be acceptable to the scientist as well as to the poet, the artist and the dreamer. In your scientific studies, as they take you deeper into the super-physical realms, be ever observant of our place in the manipulation and adjustment of nature's forces. Behind every phenomenon you will find a member of our race. Our position in nature is closely akin to that of the engineer; he is not the force himself; he directs it, and as his constant care and oversight are essential to the efficient running of the machine, so the angels, or devas,* are essential to the efficient running of the great machine of nature, as well as of each individual engine of which it is composed, from atom to archangel. So long as the presence of our invisible hosts is ignored by science there will be gaps in their knowledge, gaps which can only be filled by a comprehension of our place in the scheme of things.

That knowledge is not likely to be obtained by the use of physical instruments; and, therefore, the second essential is an increase in the number of human beings able to contact us. Perhaps the easiest means of approach will be found to be through the love of nature. Those who would find us must learn to contact nature far more intimately than is at present possible to the average man. In addition to a deeper appreciation of the beauty of nature, there

---

* Deva is a comprehensive term for the whole companion evolution, from the least nature spirit to the greatest Archangel.

must be that reverence for all forms and moods, for all her manifold expression, which springs from a recognition of the presence of the Divine of which these forms, moods and beauties are but the outward expression. From such an appreciation there will arise naturally a realisation of the sacred nature of all beauty, and a desire to draw near to the divinity within. Beyond that again, a living sense of unity with nature must be reached, till you can see yourself in every tree, in every flower, in every blade of grass, in every passing cloud, and realise that the manifold diversities which compose a valley or a garden or a wide panorama of mountain, sea and sky, are but expressions of the One Self which is in you, of which you are a part, by means of which you can pierce the external veil of beauty till it can hide from you no longer the vision of the Self. When this realisation has been gained, you will be on the threshold of our world, you will have learned to see with our eyes and to know with our minds and to feel with our hearts.

This capacity alone, however, will not suffice, for it is as yet a path which few can tread. It may, nevertheless, be regarded as the broad highway leading to the bridge.

Every true artist has gone along that road, yet few have found us; for the enquiring mind of the scientist and the penetrating gaze of the seer must be added to the sensitiveness of the artist. The scientist must learn to begin where the artist leaves off, and, placing himself within the central heart of nature, pursue his investigations outwards towards the circumference. He will not lose in his self-realisation that clarity of mind, that exactitude of observation, which he so rightly prizes, but he will direct them from a new point of view. He must place his mind *inside* the tree, the plant, the animal, the element, the atom he would study; and to do this he must first follow the path of the artist and the poet, the philosopher and the metaphysician, combining the capacities of each within himself. The realisation of the angel world will gradually begin to illumine his consciousness and, through it, every problem to which his mind is turned.

Let him first gain the necessary technique of the laboratory and the text-book, and then, forsaking these for a time, let him meditate, preferably amid the beauties of nature, appealing to us for guidance and for aid. If he be sincere, knowledge will surely come to him.

Next comes the way of ceremony, where divine ideas, words of power and precision of action are combined in a manner closely corresponding to that by which the angels work. Let all the churches and all the priests who seek this way, throw open their minds and their work to us, grant us a greater share in their beneficent activities. Members of the angel hosts are hovering over the heads of all congregations, standing beside every priest; yet how often do they find themselves shut out by barriers upraised by human minds. Let priest and congregation alike throw their minds open to a recognition of our presence in their midst, and invoke our aid; soon, very soon, some will begin to hear the beating of our wings, to feel an added power in their work, and, later, an increasing happiness in their lives. Like Him Who has come, we bring the message of happiness—we, who are expressions of bliss divine, we for whom pain is not, nor sorrow, nor parting, nor death, nor any injury, but only joy, light and ever-increasing power, as we learn to express more and more of that Will Divine from which we sprang.

For us, the cornucopia of life is ever full to overflowing and from its abundance we would feed humanity. The happiness which never fades, but grows until it becomes an ecstasy of bliss, shall be theirs. Preach, then, ye ministers of God, the Gospel of Happiness, in His Name and in ours. Would you but throw open the doors of your hearts and minds to us, doors which, in spite of the ancient teaching of your faiths, are fast locked against us, we would fill your churches, mosques and temples.

The healer, too, might invoke us to come to his aid. The sick beds of men call us, who know no pain. Wonders of healing might be performed if we might come freely. To attain this end, you must combine healing with religion, with ceremonial, as well as with the artist's vision of reality. In every institution for the care of the young, the sick and the aged, there should be established a magnetic centre which we could use as a focus: it should be a room set apart and made beautiful, consecrated by the proper ceremonial, which would have as its object the invocation of Raphael and his healing angels, and of establishing an atmosphere in which they could work. No great gift of knowledge would be needed to do this, only sincerity and vision; the room might be shaped like an octagon, with an altar towards the East, candles and the symbols of the religion of the country placed thereon, and a figure of the founder of their Faith, incense, holy water and fragrant flowers. Every morning a ceremony of invocation of the angels should be performed, and every evening a service of thanksgiving.* In every ward or sick-room, a little shrine might be similarly consecrated and similarly employed. Then every doctor would become a priest, every nurse an acolyte; we should come and heal through them, helping in a hundred ways.

In the home-life of man a place for us might be found. In some countries, the people invite our presence, but even there, from long continued usage, old customs have lost their life, remaining largely as empty forms. Adaptations suited to western civilisation might well be devised by those who wish to cross the bridge into our world.

Again, perhaps, the most suitable method would be the provision of a shrine set apart and used exclusively for invocations and offerings to the angels. In all times of need, sudden crises, sicknesses, births, and deaths, the aid of the Angels would be

---

* See Chapter XIII.

gladly given, but the power would be greater and the presences more real if magnetised centres were provided in the home. A single object of great beauty, mentally associated with the angels and with nature, a bowl of flowers, freshly gathered every day, incense, the use of a short prayer or invocation each morning, and a benediction each evening, would suffice. Complete cleanliness, an atmosphere of utter purity, and the single motive of co-operation for mutual help, are essential; while added to the simple ceremony might be an appropriate reference to the Founder of the religion of the house, and a prayer, perhaps, for His Blessing upon both angels and men.

These few examples will be sufficient to suggest a general method of communion and co-operation, for which variations may be devised for particular purposes; for example, in the studio of the artist, the surgery, the consulting room, the concert hall, the lecture room; everywhere, in fact, where angels may be usefully employed. Further fields of mutual co-operation await us in the realms of horticulture and agriculture.

While these practices would not immediately produce a large number of people capable of entering into direct communication with the angels— even if this were desirable or necessary—they would gradually effect a change in the consciousness of the people, a change which would tend to make such communication more easily possible. This development would show itself particularly among the children, who, growing up in such an atmosphere, would have every facility for developing and using powers of communication.

Many other beneficial results might be expected, culminating in a general raising of the whole tone of human life and thought, which would tend to become more sensitive, refined and responsive, as a result of contact with angel consciousness. In time this would begin to affect the actual appearance of the physical body, as well as its movements and gestures; the arts and graces of life would begin to be more generally appreciated and expressed.

For those of humanity who find within themselves a natural response to these ideas and an instinctive desire to apply them, centres and communities for their practical use might be formed in the more remote country places. Every community or centre, formed with spiritual purposes, would find its work greatly increased in value, range and power by the recognition of the presence of angels, and the practice of co-operation with them.

This valley* is well adapted for such endeavours, and it is not unlikely that, in the near future, centres, both of the Ancient Wisdom and of the new religion, will be formed and grow here; centres in which an increasing recognition and co-operation will be obtained from both the human and angel workers. Both magnetically and historically, this valley is particularly suitable for the work; what-

---

* The valley in which the messages were received.

ever methods are attempted, their success will be greatly enhanced by co-operation. A very great readiness to combine will be shown by the angels of this district, provided always that the work has as its basis the ideals and ideas of the Ancient Wisdom.

On the physical plane, the preparation and building of the form is your work; on the inner planes, we will combine with your super-physical selves in pouring in the life, in stimulating the inner growth, in the protection of the centre from intrusion, and in the conservation of the power generated.

A centre here might serve both a working community and those who seek a retreat for meditation and study; the measure of its success will be greatly increased if the conception of human and angel co-operation is kept continually to the front and the suggestion to employ such co-operation is made to all who come within its sphere of influence. Developments might be expected which would be the provision of a sanatorium and rest house—a semi-monastic institution—as a retreat, for purposes of study, meditation and investigation, with departments for literature, arts and crafts, dramatic representations, dancing and rhythmic exercises. The successful initiation of such schemes might produce a result which would serve as a model for the establishment of similar centres in other parts of the world.

The essential factor for success in co-operation between us is the mental realisation of its possi-

bility, and the continual recollection and employ-
ment of it, in the mental world, in every piece of
work which is undertaken. Anyone who will ear-
nestly practise this will almost inevitably develop
the power to realise the presence and co-operation of
the angels, and their never failing response to calls
for aid. It should be made clear that this conception
must be preserved in its simplest form, entirely free
from all sensationalism or elaborate ceremonial,
nor is it suggested that any attempt should be made
to obtain a close personal contact with individual
angels, or to employ them from motives of personal
gain, interest or curiosity; such endeavours would
almost inevitably lead to disaster and should be rigorously excluded. It must be as natural for you to
work with the angels as with each other or with domestic animals. As already stated, the qualities of
Simplicity, Purity, Directness and Impersonality
must characterise all who hope to take part successfully in any mutual endeavours. The excitable,
emotional, or unbalanced individual may not safely
be brought into contact with the great forces working behind and through the angel evolution. Men
and women with extremely practical and controlled
minds, possessing also capacities for idealism and
positive imagination, are ideal workers; these types
should be sought for the initiation of schemes
where human-angel co-operation is to be employed.

Though the world at large may deride our aspira-
tions, a growing response is assured. There exists

within the human heart and mind an instinctive attraction in these directions; it springs in part at least from ancient memories of those times when angels walked with men, and partly from the natural seership latent in every human soul.

III
THE SECOND MESSAGE

THE Angels ask from you, not worship—for
that would be inappropriate—but love; asking
only to be allowed to join with you in praise and
thanksgiving to Him Who is the Father of us all,
and in adoration of the Supreme Teacher of Angels
and of Men. The power of our prayers will be enhanced by being offered up with yours; your lives
will be enriched by the answer to our common act
of praise. Our sphere of usefulness to God will be
enlarged by sharing yours; your lives will be enriched, your world made glad, by the inauguration
of the Brotherhood of Angels and of Men. The aim
of the Brotherhood is to widen the range of human
love by including the angels within its rosy glow, so

25

that the concept of brotherhood, the keynote of the coming age, shall know no bounds, but widen to include all living things, mortal and immortal—the dwellers in the ethereal worlds of air, fire and water —the people of the limitless dominions of Space.

The time approaches when they will no longer remain invisible to you, for as you throw open your worlds to them, so will they cease to resist your entry into theirs; throwing wide their doors they will invite you to pass the portal, offering you full share of those treasures of incalculable value which they have guarded so long. It is love that will open the doors; love between yourselves first, so that you can never misuse the gifts they will bestow; love also for them, your brethren, to whom your love will give the power to reveal themselves. The angels send their love and greeting to you, holding out their hands in fellowship, as bidden by the Lord. Surrounded by angels, as of old, He comes, and we, His servants, bear His message of brotherhood and love, "Be of the same mind, one with another, for there is but one Life, boundless and inexhaustible, which is the very essence of you all. Go to the children of men, draw close to them once more, that those days may be brought back again when angels walked with men. Do this, it is the Will of God."

Having this command laid upon us we come to you, and to many another listening one, offering you our service and our love, that His Will be done.

What will your answer be, men of earth?

We wait on that. We would light a fire in your hearts that you may feel the glow of the same great flame that burns within us, the flame of divine Life, that restores as it consumes, ever renewing its fiery power in the lives of those in whom it burns. That is the meaning of the angel life, this is the secret of the angel fire, the fire divine which burns continually; it is the flame which leaps from that immortal spark, our innermost Selves, which springs from the central fiery heart of the universe—the Spiritual Sun.

All your faculties will be increased, and all your powers enhanced, till life becomes an ecstasy, till unsuspected beauty reveals itself in everything, till undreamed-of capacity for love, for life, for happiness, arises within you. Thus you shall find your way to that Kingdom of Happiness, of ecstasy, of bliss, to which our Lord in His divine compassion would lead you.

All this, and more, awaits you in the future, a future that shall be near or far according to your response to Him and to His angel hosts. He desires to open a new world to you—new yet older than yourselves—to open to you Kingdoms yet invisible; He will remove the scales from your eyes, and the vision splendid will be yours.

Come into that Kingdom, the land of immortality in which we dwell, and share with us the joys which never fail, the splendours of a world where death is unknown, where separation is not, nor any pain. Let the beauty, the power and the joy of the vision flow down into your world, healing its distress, relieving its drudgery, ugliness and vice, that all men may lift up their heads in pride, having once more become the gods they ought to be.

Begone the sunken eye, the withered cheek, the scowling glance, the shamed mien, the ugly home. Let Life be beautiful for all, not for the few alone; for He Who comes, comes to all, and He would remove these dark blots upon your race, for He sees the God within you struggling to be free.

These lives—dark, drear, dull as the tomb—must be made glad, must be filled with joy, must be given the freedom which He bids you give.

Raise up the evolving god; do not press Him down or bury Him deeper and deeper in the mire of your own selfishness. So shall all be lifted up, a fairer race shall be born, a nobler type evolve, and a more worthy temple be reared of human bodies, happy, healthy, strong and free, fit dwellings for the God hidden within them.

He comes to help you to this end. To help you and Him we come, offering ourselves to you. We, who have not felt the cramping and deadening weight of earth, honour you for your great pilgrimage so far from His Face—from Whom you sprang —so deep into the dense material worlds. Now that your faces are turned homeward, He bids us sing the welcoming song; He bids us meet you on the way, and, joining hands with you, lead you more swiftly along the Path of Return back to His abode, the Dwelling Place of Light.

IV

THE HIGHEST

THERE is too much satisfaction with that which
is not the highest, and not enough readiness to
aim higher and higher still in all things that are
done. Even in the pleasant talk of friends, there
should always be upheld the ideal that thought and
word and deed should be *the highest;* because this
is not so, the keen edge of heart and mind is
blunted, the sense of greatness falls away, lesser
things come into and clog the soul, delaying its
progress on the Path. These things should not be,
need not be; even little things are great for those
who continually aspire. Make something great of
all things. The walk, the drive, the fireside talk, all
the household ways, all your earthly obligations,

your pleasures and your pains, your strivings and your times of ease—let them be great, the greatest that, so far, has dawned within you—the highest you can reach.

Let this be the motto for you all—THE HIGHEST—and let all who join our ranks pledge themselves to that motto. We, too, will pledge ourselves, and every time this inward pledge is uttered by a man, an angel shall repeat his pledge and bear it like a torch to add to the great reservoir of power apportioned for our work. Let each who would so pledge himself, retire into solitude, the private room, some grassy height, some woodland shade, or, if he needs them not, into the chamber of his heart. There with fixed purpose let him first meditate, seeking to penetrate into the depth and meaning of our great ideal; then, having envisaged it, let him make firm resolve that he will ever strive towards it throughout this and his future lives; remembering that to the great all things are great.

Thus, perchance, we may remove the blight that threatens your race, the blight of apathy; in which you are sunk so deep that only wars, earthquakes, fires and floods, famines and sudden death can stir your somnolence. Your higher selves—your angel selves—strive continually to awaken you, to send a vision through your dreams, and here and there a sleeper stirs and stretches, all too often to return to sleep; your dreams must be disturbed by the force of things external to your selves. Wars come to rouse you, and you pray to God to save you from more wars! Pestilence and famine stride hand in hand across your heedless lives, and only as you see them threatening your repose do you awake, and, for a time, become your greatest selves. Yet from these, you pray unto your Lord, asking Him to deliver you! The deliverer from these is with you all the while, it is your innermost self; but as you will not be aroused by the Self within you, you must be awakened by the Self without. Know that in wars, plagues, cataclysms, you see yourselves, the expressions of your soul, striding torch in hand, through the dormitories in which your bodies lie, to stir you from your sleep, to drive away the dark shadows of self-satisfaction and content. These other selves of yours will come again and again until you yourselves banish them for all time. They go from the nation, from those men, who, answering to the highest, live according to its laws; who seeing the greatest, strive ever to express it, who neither rest nor sleep, filled with a craving which drives them onwards from peak to peak of the mountains of the spiritual world. That is the way to release, brothers, and there is none other. He who tells you that war may cease by act of law, does worse than lie; he covers up the truth, so that men, feeling safe, sink back again into their dreams—and war returns in due season.

In our Brotherhood, we must begin to hold aloft this great ideal—THE HIGHEST—and each must pledge himself that nothing else will satisfy his soul. You must preach this gospel—that the cause of all things, good and ill, lies within ourselves, that the good may be made better and the bad disappear, only by action from within. It is the *lives* of men you must reform, not their laws; lives can only change when they conform to the highest, instead of trifling with the lowest.

No man can plead that he does not know these things. Messenger after messenger has come and spread the truth abroad. It is you who have locked up such truths in temple, church, and mosque, and taken refuge in the courts of law, till self-denial is unknown, and is displaced by denial of the Self. Still you laugh contemptuously, when told that love shall save the world—or purity, or truth, or law, or sacrifice. You have hardened your hearts; yet He still comes, the embodiment of love, purity and truth, of law and sacrifice, to teach you once again the ancient truths, lest war—an even greater war—should take His place as Teacher of Angels and of Men.

Let this be our motto and our password, the sign by which we know each other by day and night—THE HIGHEST. Seek an artist friend that he may draw a picture of a member of the angel host standing upon a globe and pointing to the sky, and underneath—"THE HIGHEST." Call it "The Angel of the Pointing Hand"; make it into badge and talisman, bless it with power and love and courage to achieve, that all who wear it may be filled with divine discontent and a craving for the highest, a longing for the goal. Learn to make the form in the mental worlds and fill it with your desire, and send it out to men. Charge it to the full with your will; call upon an angel to ensoul it with his life, until you fill the mental world with glowing forms of angel kind which shall call to the mental selves of men, shall wake them from their sleep. Flood the mental world with this ideal, the ideal of THE HIGH-EST.

V

PATIENCE

CAN you conceive an eagerness to work, so great that even our bodies seem near to breaking under its power, yet an eagerness combined with patience that can wait a thousand years? To that sublime patience you must attain, for within the quality of patience is enclosed a multitude of virtues, strength to control, power to restrain, vision of the Plan, knowledge of the real, detachment from results and co-ordination of the will, the mind, the body, so that when the time comes they act as one. Patience of this kind does not extinguish the fire of eagerness to serve, rather does it glow ever more fiercely within the compression exercised by will and mind. When at last the order comes, when, after the passing of an age, the day arrives when the restraints are to be released, then it is that the power stored up for so long flashes forth through us. We become the catapults of God.

Now that day has come, stored-up energies, resulting from the power of the great ideal, have been released into your world. Fear not the result; the end is sure. Not for nought have your Hierarchy and ours planned, from time beyond your power to count, ever waiting for the arrival of the day; so I say the end is sure. Still they plan, for ages yet unborn, great schemes, embodying the divine Will; in detail, too, down to the angels and the men they choose. What, then, are we but incidents, straws, blown by the breath of God, except that within those straws the self-same breath is found, so that breath answers to breath, and His Will is done.

Remember always that the ultimate source of power is in the idea, the power we use in manifested worlds is but the force emanating from and the reflection of the divine Idea. If this be true, then no delay can reduce its potency, nor any circumstance prevent its ultimate expression. Upon this knowledge should patience be based.

VI
PEACE

PEACE is an essential principle in nature, not merely a quality to be acquired; it belongs to the innate essence of all things, and, like love, is a cohesive principle. Behind all movement there is rest; behind all sound there is stillness; so that behind the motion and the music of the spheres there is peace—the equipoise of God. Though all His planets and all His people move, He is motionless, and nought is there within His wide dominions that can disturb His peace, so firmly founded. You, too, if you would achieve, must find that peace, that power of divine equipoise which nothing in the outer world can shake, which no untoward circumstance can destroy. I would have you turn your

36

thoughts to this great discovery, the discovery of that within yourselves which is a reflection of the peace of God. It is not your own, it is not a quality which you will acquire; it is a power that you will release; it is the gyroscopic centre of your soul. At first it is like an isolation of the soul, so deep is its stillness, so utterly devoid of sound.

The way to this realm of peace lies through the mind, for the roads which lead towards its boundaries are paved with thought; over those roads the soul must tread. Therefore, by thought you must begin. Think frequently of peace; mistake it not for quiet, nor any condition of external things, however noiseless, however still; you must plunge deeper, into the innermost recesses of the soul, in quest of the land of peace. It is not of the mind nor of the heart, though the essence of both is rooted deep within it. Meditate on peace, thus will you pave the road which you must tread later, so that it be smooth and easy for your feet; as you walk and near the frontier, the sense of manifested life will gradually fall away, you will feel alone. Fear not, 'tis but the aura of the land of peace which stretches far and wide and meets you on the road; enter it, and let its power strengthen you for the later stages of the quest; as the stillness deepens round you, welcome it and let it permeate your soul, till every nerve, ever atom, seems to find rest.

Mistake not this deep reflection for the goal itself, as many have done; peace lies still deeper, the innermost recesses must be explored; even while all nature seems to pause, and the goal almost to be won, press on your quest. The drawbridge is down, the portcullis raised; press on, for, compared to the peace which now awaits you, that which you just have known is as discord and turmoil, as far from reality as earthly fire is from the spiritual sun, yet related to it, and therefore to be encountered on the way; it was external peace and not your own. Pass then through the gates, and be lost in that which is yourself; fall into the abyss, plunge into the pool, which, though it seems but nothingness, is everything—the pool of peace.

Think deeply on these words, my brothers, and try the quest. It is part of our angel discipline, the schooling of the angel hosts; lacking the anchorage which your earthly bodies give to you, the devas are useless in great tasks till they have found that stable point within their inmost depths, which serves them, as your bodies serve your minds, for leverage; lacking flesh, they have to find the fulcrum deep within. Why should you not find it, too, and, having both the inner fulcrum and the flesh, preserve that outer poise unshakeable which is the expression of spiritual peace, the final, deepest point of self, beyond which self is not?

It was from this source, so deep within, that the power was released which the raging tempest on the Galilean sea could not gainsay; it was from that land that He spoke, saying unto wind and wave: "Peace, be still." Though it is no earthly peace, it wields a power that all earthly things must own—

resistless in its might. When He gave His peace to His own, saying: "Not as the world giveth, give I," He spoke from that same inner land. Thence came also the power which, through His music, tamed the wildest and most warlike creatures of the Thracian wilds, which drew down the branches of the trees and held them still, which forced the lion and the tiger and the snake to lose their fierceness and their lust and become quiet, for Orpheus sang, "Peace, be still." And ever, where His presence is, there is peace—there motion seems to cease.

So, He who lives forever in that land of eternal equipoise, comes bringing peace, and as He, coming thence, brings peace to the world, so may you— drawing on the self-same source, the deepest point, the stable point, the point of rest within yourselves —find peace, and the warfare of your lower selves will cease. You too must acquire the magic of that far-off land which shall give to your voice the power to say "Peace, be still." None living in these outer worlds can resist that power; the wildest sylph, the fiercest creature of the fire, the elementals of the storm, the earthquake, the volcano, and the flood, must stay their mighty onrush, their resistless, vivid play, at the command of him who can truly say "Peace, be still."

This peace is the essence of all beautiful things. The quiet hour, the peaceful scene, the home fireside, the clasping hands of those who love, the worship of the devotee, the adoration of the saint, the blessing of the Gods—all these have as their essence, peace, and without peace their beauty is gone. Therefore, win peace.

Your peoples have so much which would be beautiful but is not, for want of peace; you ape the beautiful yet achieve it not, for want of peace; nearly all your art is spoiled by too much striving and by want of peace. Only the greatest of your men of fire have truly achieved great art, great in the measure of peace it enshrines; yet everything that grows—the gem, the rose, the weed, the insect, the animal, the man—is beautiful. All are the achievements of an art which springs from peace—like lotus flowers, resting on the surface of the pool.

O, my brothers, if you would but give the world this one message, asking men to seek peace; not the freedom from the clash of arms, not absence of civil or industrial strife, not lessening of the claims from man to man, for these are but the husks, the chaff, which flies into the air at the grinding of the karmic mills. If you would escape the karmic debt of war, you must lead the souls of men to that land of spiritual peace, in which to contemplate and find, each for himself, the Peace Divine.

If you would but emulate the silent-footed devas of the air, who live their lives, not in soundlessness, but in song; whose every moment is a harmony, whose every thought paints a bright picture on the canvas of the sky, whose very heartbeats are whisperings of joy! When you tell men that we come, ask them this boon in our name—that they will cultivate peace. Life must, indeed, be motion, and motion sound; but let all the sounds of human life bring harmony, and let them learn to make their path melodious and sweet. Teach them to listen to the music of the trees, show them the way firs and pines and beeches live, swaying to the wind and singing all the time. They have swayed and sung since Time was; now they are incapable, in any circumstances, of stridency or discord in their song.

So near, oft-times, do we come, hoping that you will hear the beating of our wings, and yet we fail, and often must retire, driven away, almost with horror, at the sounds and forms emitted by your ways of living. Appeal for the abolition of every sound which might hurt the ear of a child, in city, in street, in country lane, in factory, farm, or field, so that gradually you will have removed this impassable barrier of noise, which you have erected between our world and yours. Teach your people to cultivate the quiet hour, to learn the joy of peace, the mood of silent happiness, for these are the obvious ways of human life, these should be the natural expression of your lives; if you have not attained to these how can we teach the deeper paths of peace, the super-human way, how lead you past your normal selves into the land where God is seen, walking in His garden of peace?

Inaugurate a great campaign, bid all those who come later to help, that this great wave of ugliness and violence shall pass, for this chance is an essential preliminary to the realisation of our mutual ideals. Though ordered by the Prince of Peace, though filled with the love of the Lord of Love, we cannot come until you quieten all your lives and listen to our knock upon your door, to our footfall beside your hearths. Discord and ugliness must vanish from the world; to remove it is our task and yours—but yours first. Rewards are promised, even at the beginning of your task, for you shall hear such music, you shall see such beauty as will exceed your noblest dreams, when we come bearing our gifts to men—gifts that can be given only to a world ready to receive them, gifts that cannot be withheld, when once the preparation has been made; for, throughout all time, these have been the gifts of the angels—music and beauty; every quality and every movement of the God within the angel finds expression through these. Love, one for another, between us, shows itself in bursts of song; with us, great thoughts are symphonies; and, as we answer love to love, and thought to thought, all the air about us is filled with tones and supertones, with harmonies, songs, chants and great chorales; not manufactured as something to show our gifts, but as beauties which cannot be withheld, beauties which spring forth full-born, natural expressions of our intercourse, our lives of love and labour, in our own world.

You, too, make pictures every time you think; you, too, make music every time you feel, and light and colour and form as well; and these things might shine resplendent and beautiful in your world, the beauty of their music might fill your ears. These things are all about you, modified, it is true, but you know them not. You do not live for beauty, your lives are not spent ever listening for a song; furthermore, you spoil your songs, your forms, your light, by greed and selfishness and vice. These errors would quickly vanish if you but heard and saw the monstrous sounds and sights that spring from them.

Seeing all we see, do you wonder that the angels weep, beholding Gods fallen so low?

VII
EDUCATION

THIS is the way of the teacher; first to uplift the soul; secondly, to expand the mind; thirdly, to vivify the understanding; and fourthly, to co-ordinate body, mind and soul.

To teach you, I must first call you up into the land of joy,* that you may stand in the presence of knowledge.

Knowledge is truth arranged in sequences; knowledge is truth mirrored in the human soul; knowledge is the life-aspect of learning—the twain should never be confused. Knowledge is the syn-

---

* See Chapter VIII.

thesis of all that learning gives; knowledge is unity as it finds expression in the realm of ideas.

Knowledge differs from wisdom. Wisdom ever grows, knowledge is stationary; wisdom is the self of knowledge, knowledge is wisdom expressed as ideas; wisdom is innate within the human soul, the human soul must acquire knowledge. When knowledge is gained, it is no longer required; knowledge is only useful as a key to unlock the hidden wisdom. Knowledge belongs to the unreal; wisdom to the real. Knowledge dies, wisdom is eternal; knowledge is the odour, wisdom is the flower; knowledge is light, wisdom is the sun; knowledge is the picture, wisdom is the vision, the soul of man is the artist.

To the teacher, the pupil is the artist who will translate wisdom to knowledge after he has found wisdom through knowledge. The teacher must teach wisdom, not knowledge. The mission of the teacher is to elevate the pupil, to place him in the presence of knowledge, that he may reach out his hand to such knowledge, as he may desire—the teacher watching all the while, guiding the selection, influencing the expression, of that which is acquired. When the pupil is familiar with knowledge, the teacher shows him how to use it as a key with which to unlock the hidden wisdom. As the doors swing wide and wisdom is revealed, the teacher withdraws; thereafter watches from afar.

Wisdom cannot be revealed until the soul is lifted

up; therefore, let all teachers-to-be learn first to lift up the souls of men.

Teaching should begin by prayer, so that the pupil may learn to free his soul from earthly things. Being free, he must mount on wings of prayer, that his soul may be lifted up. Having lifted him to heights where knowledge dwells, the teacher should support the pupil, holding him by the hand until he learns the equipoise of that unaccustomed land. Then, and then only, may the teacher begin to teach.

There is but one way to teach; that is by sharing, for that is the way God teaches, and every teacher should be to his pupil as a God. The art of teaching is the art of God; that is His purpose in His universe, to educate. All teachers should aspire to be Godlike, for, being Gods in miniature, all their work becomes divine.

The teachers of a nation should be its noblest sons, its greatest men. They should learn to elevate their souls, should find those hidden pathways through the mind which lead from brain to wisdom, from wisdom back to brain. They should use these daily, till all the ways of flesh, of feeling, thought, ideas and wisdom, are as familiar lands. The teacher must survey these lands, each in its turn, until he has distilled the essence of them all, has learned to stand and to be free in each world. Then, and only then, can he truly educate. Then only can he guide his pupil's feet along the path which he has trodden, then leave the pupil free to use the pathway for himself.

For the teacher, wisdom is the highest; for the pupil, will. The teacher should not begin to teach until he has touched the highest, lest he should err in the lowest. But, having learned the secret whereby wisdom is revealed, and having kept the pathway free, seated in wisdom, he can order all his actions in the lower world according to wisdom's decree. Then will he be worthy to teach, for wisdom cannot err.

With wisdom he will examine his pupil's body, especially the brain, the organ with which he is concerned; he will order all the pupil's earthly life, that brain and body may be developed to express wisdom; for nothing less should be his aim. The body must be supple, loose and free; the brain elastic, sensitive, responsive to what is high, unresponsive to what is low. Carefully, day by day, nay, even hour by hour, the teacher should watch the growth of the body and of brain. The earthly life should be suffused continually with joy; he should not permit even the shadow of a pain, for pain is the teacher of maturity, pain is the teacher of the pupil's later years, not of his youth.

The qualities of joy and freedom must be developed to the utmost in the child; this is essential to ultimate success. Failing this, growth will be warped, body and brain will harden, the higher faculties be dulled. All the food and clothing of the child must be light, yet containing also the elements of strength. Purity should surround him from his birth; all that is gross should be rigorously kept away. Thus only may the body grow to be light and strong, pure, joyous and free. Having these, the basic factors of his growth, all else will follow naturally; virtue will develop, vice will gain no hold.

On these, the teacher's basic principles, the curriculum should be based. If the child should err, let the teacher blame himself; he has not taught aright, he has failed to share; failing to share means that he has not loved. Without love, no man should begin to teach. As God watches the growth of His universe, sharing with it His life, His wisdom and His joy, so must the teacher, meditating continually, sharing his vision and his wisdom with the pupil. As he sees his many pupils grow in earthly strength and grace, in mental gifts, in heavenly wisdom, he should pay close attention to the diversities of gifts and character which each one develops as he grows; for only by close study and wise discrimination can he select each one and place him in his natural group so that classes may be formed; for only those should be grouped whose gifts and character demand a similarity of method.

One of the most difficult and important tasks of the teacher is the grouping of the pupils in the class. He should not group so much by age or subject to be taught as by innate character. When thus the proper groups are formed, they may be mingled or even interchanged, but in all that affects the close relation between the teacher and the taught, a proper grouping should be maintained. So also, in the world of thought and feeling; it is with the highest wisdom that the underlying bases of the teacher's art should be applied. When the teacher imparts knowledge, he should at the same time show the pupil how he may acquire that knowledge for himself. Thus it is that, when I lift you to the land of joy and make you free in all its wide domain, I show you also how to open wide your eyes, that for yourself you may see; for this is the teacher's way.

VIII

JOY

I WOULD sing to you of joy, the joy of the Gods
as they revel in the land of joy.
The land of joy is the land of dreams, where every
dream comes true,
Where every thought and answering thought thrills
with joy.
The land of joy is the land of the Gods, there lives
the God in man;
For men are Gods, and the Godly part dwells in the
land of the Gods.
The land of joy is beyond the mind, through the
gates of eternal peace.
Angels share that land with men, and these are the
Gods who sing;

Thrills of gladness fill the air, by joy we live and
    breathe;
Everything there is full of joy, like the bursting buds
    of spring;
Throughout all the land is the freshness of morn, of
    dew, of bud, of flower.
Lightly the angels pass on their way, wafted on
    wings of joy;
Nature wears a perennial smile, a smile that is ever
    new;
Laughter rings through the woods and dells, for the
    joy of eternal spring.

All power, all truth, all vision, all work, all life,
are expressed in that land in terms of joy. An effort
of will sends a wave of gladness through that land;
new tasks are welcomed with the smile of those
who greet their dearest friend. Every heart and
every soul thrills with the dancing gladness of
spring; vast choirs of angels sing songs of joy.
Cherubim and Seraphim disport themselves, their
winged faces shining with joy. In that land every
thought becomes a poem.

The lower man must join the higher man in the
land of joy; the twain must walk together through
its green places. The higher man is calling, ever
calling to the lower: "Come, come into the land of
joy." As his eyes are opened, splendour on splendour is revealed. The fluting pipes of Seraphim, the
treble songs of Cherubim—those twins sing and
play in concert in the land of joy. No earthly eyes

can see, no earthly ears may hear, the vision and the music of this land; no earthly hand of lower man can ever truly write its wonder and beauty, its ecstasy and thrilling gladness. It is the land where every earthly happiness finds birth; a single thrill within it gives birth unto a thousand happy hours in the world below. Its wayside flowers are parents of earth's most luscious blooms; its trees, waving in the evening breeze, send divine melodies to the lower ears of men.

Springlike freshness of air, lily-scented bowers, oceans wide like mighty frosted panes, reflecting the noon-day sun, rivers of crystal, streamlets whose waters are of precious stones, waterfalls and cataracts like broken sun-rays flashing through a thousand prisms, billowy foam, showers of spray of diamonds, each drop lighted with an inward sun, tall trees, like stately mothers of the Gods emerald clad; clouds that are alive and gambol like the lambs as they float across a sky of sweeping vastness with ever changing hues, lighted as if by a thousand sunsets; air balmy, buoyant and full of song like the trickling of a rill, air of particles which constantly explode and shed bright radiance, vitality and all the fresh odours of spring—of such is the land of joy.

It is a land of fair valleys, towering heights, vast chasms, great precipices, every rock and stone be-jewelled with a thousand gems; earth that is pig-ment reflecting the hues of the sky; each particle of earth a separate life, a pulsing, heart-shaped diamond, translucent, yet full of colour and of light. Every shade that passes over the sky changes the colour of the earth, is broken to a thousand hues by myriads of nature's prisms. There are no deserts there, yet all the land is like an oasis, a mirage that is true.

In that land, so far and yet so near, the immortal self of man resides. There all day long he walks, companioned by his angel kin, each ensouled by joy, each its embodiment. There distance is not, for all the world is at his feet; there no time passes, for eternity is his. Such is the land wherein the souls of men dwell; such is man's spiritual home.

Though I speak of land, of river, sea and sky, of trees that wave majestically, of precipices and glade, of mountain-top and field, it is but the essence of these things, and not their form, which compose the varied landscape of the land of joy. For it is the land of light, where all things are of light; there is no form that you would recognise as form; yet form is known through cognizance of the essence of all form. Beauty gives ecstasy, the answering thrill of joy, yet it is not beauty's form but beauty's self we see. In this world of eternal gladness, there are no words, for the soul of men and angels have no need of words, nor are there thoughts, for thoughts are but divisions of ideas, as words are but divisions of thoughts. Here division cannot be, for the land of joy is unity made manifest, yet not in form.

Unity is the basic law of the land of joy. All the

knowledge that men acquire by thought is here, without the need of thought; all the deepest love they ever feel is here, universally shining, not from a centre or a part, but implicit throughout. The music that you know by thought, by feeling and by sound is a faint and far-off echo of its universal music. Before this music could find true expression in the lower worlds, every atom of the worlds of thought, of feeling and of flesh, would have to learn to sing, so that there would be no room at all for anything save music; even the interstices between the particles which build the form would be filled with song. Before the lower man could hear the wondrous sound, he must be built anew, of singing atoms, so that he could hear the atom's universal song. Yet, even then, for him the vision and the sound of the land of joy would be afar off; for in that land, thought, love, beauty and music are one and indivisible, interchangeable, each instinct with the other; inseparable is this four-fold life-force, yet one.

Every human ideation in the lower worlds is here a living thing, completely comprehended in a flash in all its possibilities, from birth to ultimate expression and full maturity, and beyond that to the fading of the power, even to its death. Birth, maturity, death, here the three are known as one. In this land where joy reigns, dwell the ideations of the universe; they are the essence, distilled drop by drop from the consciousness of God; here, the immortal self of man sheds upon the lower man the odours of those precious essences, the scents of those perfumes. As the lower man, in world of thought, breathes their delicious scent, a system of philosophy is born, a symphony formed, a mighty flood of genius released.

The creative fire which drives the artist on is fed from the petals of the flowers from which these perfumes are distilled, for earthly flowers are but the solid embodiment of universal ideations. In the land of joy there is but one perfume—the essence of every odour of the world below, containing all. Angels descending to the lower worlds where heavenly joy will one day reign, bear in their hands, censers, exhaling perfumes from above, and, as they fly, they swing them, pervading the world of thought and feeling with their power. As the thinking and feeling selves of men breathe in the scented power, great deeds of heroism and love are born in worlds of flesh. The mother clasps the babe more closely to her breast, ready to give her life for it, if need be. Round her the angels gather, and flood her with their perfume. In the morning she wakes with courage all renewed, to continue the hourly heroism of her daily life. Of that heroism the angels sing, and the song is heard in the land of joy; and the immortal self smiles, knowing that the time shall quickly come when the lower and the higher shall be one, knowing that his earthly pilgrimage shall yield most precious fruit, that his earthly "son" shall come home, laden with gifts, gifts that will add new splendour, new gladness and new power to the ecstasy by which he finds expression in the land of joy.

To every man and woman in every walk of life in the lower worlds, the angels come, bearing their perfume, the aroma of eternal ecstasy. They would waken in the hearts of every man, a craving for that scent, would give to men the knowledge that they have a heavenly home, would show them in the mirror of the mind the reflection of their heavenly self—the vision of their own immortality.

This is the mission, also, of every teacher among men, every preacher, healer, sage, artist, scientist, statesman and king. All have as their mission, if they but rightly understood it, to reveal to man his own inherent splendour, to lead him through the sorrows of his earthly life back to his spiritual home, the land of joy.

IX

VISION

ALL labour should be performed in the light of vision, and none undertaken until vision has been achieved. However well plans may be laid, they will fail unless they are based upon vision. Vision is relative, and a question of degrees. It is not fixed, but changes as the minutes pass and must therefore be renewed constantly. Vision is the contact of the small self with the great Self. It is the knowledge of divine ideas.

Before the birth of stars, before the growth of worlds, came vision—before all things manifest and unmanifest is vision. Vision comes before the first act of God; it is the life of the unmanifest, and the world in which it dwells. Vision reveals the plan; is the essence of the real, that from which it sprang, and that by which it grew, that by which its ultimate expression is achieved. Vision regulates the march of the spheres, guides the universe, rules the Cosmos; behind all the multitude of stars and worlds, throughout the infinities of space is vision. If you delve into the innermost heart of God, you will find Him seated in the midst of vision—vision which is the heart of the real; from His vision proceeds the real, and from the real the unreal.

Vision passes to manifestation through the unmanifest, and if you would escape the confines of the universe, seeking the Cosmos, searching for the Absolute—what you will find is vision: so vast, so all-embracing, so infinite, that to you it will appear as darkness, darkness from which you will shrink; a darkness and a silence so profound as to exclude all possibility of light and sound, a stillness so absolute as to exclude the possibility of motion.

Such is the vision of the Absolute. Your wings may not carry you across its wide spaces; you cannot fall into its dark depths, your eyes cannot penetrate its utter blackness, wings, eyes and voice serve you no longer, you must turn backward, craving for sound and light and motion. Yet that which to you is positive negation, is the vision from which all universes spring. Descend, then, once more, to your own world, finding there a reflection of the darkness you can comprehend, for even as you gaze into its depths, vision will come, and you will know all that has been, is, and is to be—the vision of the Now, that which is behind eternity.

No man possesses it, no ruler, even of systems or of worlds, can claim it for their own, since they themselves are but the shadows appearing within its dark depths. Yet it is not evanescent, nor aerial, nor ethereal, nor does it ever change; IT IS.

The highest point within you is but a reflection of that vision; every cell in every world is ordered by it. You and I and all that live are ordered by that vision in our enfolding and unfolding. It is not God, for God Himself, whether He be man, angel, world, or ruler of worlds, or even ruler of rulers of worlds, must conform to it. Whence it came is not known, nor ever could be known, for it is behind all knowledge, even of the Supreme. It is at once apex and base, and sides of the pyramid of all things manifest and unmanifest. When men, angels, worlds, and rulers of worlds, pass from manifestation to the unmanifest again, vision remains; nor is it changed in its varying decrees.

So, my brothers, in all things let us seek the vision. Whenever our eyes rest upon a form, let us seek its vision; and when we hear a sound, or see a light, or grasp an idea, or even for a brief space touch reality, let us remember that behind all these there is vision, and, remembering, bend our powers with tireless search, to find it; since when it is found, the key of knowledge is revealed. It is not here, nor there, nor anywhere, but everywhere.

When you gaze on beauty, you gaze upon the Self, and when you gaze upon the Self you see yourself; and behind the greater and the lesser selves is vision. The vision that you have, the dreams of future lives, the splendour of great plans, the inward urge to tread the path, to find the goal, the craving of your hearts to make a perfect world, to heal the sick, to appease all pain, to annihilate the ignorance of man—the vision of all this in you, is a faint reflection of the vision seen by That which is the summation of all that is. For behind That too is vision.

There is a graded order, including all visions, great and small. Remember this, and ever seek to test your own small share, raising it stage by stage through the graded orders which lead from the unreal to the real, and from the real to vision. Just as no vision you can have is comparable to that of the ruler of your worlds, so is His vision not to be compared with that from which it springs. In all your lives, in all the worlds, seek vision. Behind the atom and the gem, behind the growing plant and mighty tree, behind the fawn, the lion and the tiger too, behind the angel and the man, behind archangels and Solar Lords—is vision; until you have found it your soul will not find rest. Sight, even mental sight, is to it as the ideas of a world to the infinitude of ideations behind all worlds. Yet sight is the instrument by which it may be known; for there is a graded order of sight, a stairway of vision, winding in a never-ending spiral through all worlds and through all space; somewhere, on one step of that infinitely splendid spiral way is physical sight; next above is mental sight, the vision of the mind, and, beyond that, spiritual sight, which leads to universal sight and thence to Cosmic sight and, beyond that, unknown sight—unknown save that there is no end, that somewhere in that unknown infinitude the highest and the lowest meet. There is nought separating the highest sight from the lowest, nor are they different save as they show themselves in each individual soul.

This is the starting point for every quest, that, inasmuch as it can show itself through us, everything is ours; for within man too, that mighty spiral can be found, not *of* him, but passing *through* him, winding its way from below, entering his feet, as it were, and winding through him till it passes out above his head into his deeper self. These spirals pass through all things, as all things must climb up them within themselves. These lesser spirals are, to the mighty curves of the Cosmic stairs, as are its circular reflections to the rainbow—not the rainbow itself, but expressions of its light. Behind the lesser and the greater curves is vision—vision of the spiral whole.

X

THOROUGHNESS

IF you find and tread this pathway, see that every-thing you do is done with thoroughness and efficiency. Absence of thoroughness is a denial of divinity. As divinity is implicit throughout the universe, so should thoroughness be implicit throughout your work. Set a standard for yourselves. Absence of thoroughness means loss of force, since without it no work can be clear-cut in its outlines, finished in its expression. Work should be regarded as a vessel containing force; the force of the idea behind it. Thoroughness gives to the vessel a perfect outline. Where the outline of a form is perfect, there is no loss of force. Work should be regarded as a chalice held up to the mind, that through the mind, the power of the idea of which the work is the ultimate expression, may descend into it. If the work is not thorough, the chalice will be mal-formed, the wine spilled; therefore work always with thoroughness. So God works throughout His universe, in which there is not even the smallest part which does not bear the impress of His mind. Nothing, however minutely small, is overlooked; nothing, however great, that is not completely per-vaded by and held within the grasp of His mind. He makes of His universe a perfect chalice. Under His control no force is ever wasted. The cup of His work, full to overflowing, never overflows. So also His ministers work, the dual hierarchies of arch-angels and perfected saints, His Holy Ones, His right hand and His left.

The only ideal for which man may worthily strive is that of joining the rank of the ministers of God, whether of human or of angel kind. That ideal can only be achieved by successful imitation of Their methods. The keynote of Their work is thoroughness; let it be the keynote of yours. With-out it the highest cannot be achieved. If your work concerns the details of life, work with infinitely careful attention to detail; if you deal in broader outlines, in wider sweeps, plan with an equal thor-oughness. Thus will your work embody the power of the idea upon which it is based; thus you will achieve success.

It is essential that the idea should be true, that is, an expression of the divine idea. Then it will be a source of power, and will give a power, a dynamic energy to the work which is its ultimate expression, raising it to heights worthy of a worker who aspires to serve as the hand of God. The idea represents the head; the worker, the hand of God.

On this conception base all your work. Thus you will achieve greatness, thus you will live according to the highest, thus truth will be yours, thus you will enter the land of joy, ever to live therein, for joy and work are synonyms in the land of joy. There is no joy without work; all work is joy; therefore, my brothers, when you work, remember joy. Try to make of your world a reproduction of the land of joy. Keep joy uppermost; flood your house with joy, your garden, too. Let joyousness pervade your neighbourhood. Preach, teach, inculcate joy, set it upon high, hold it up before the eyes of men, become yourselves its embodiments. Thus will you bring the sense of the land of joy even to the earthly hearts and minds of men.

Cease to divide your world and work into compartments; train yourselves to see in everything an expression of the One. Practise the discovery of synonyms, play at matching them. Do not pass from work to play, from play to prayer, from prayer to worship in your Church, from Church to recreation; do all things as from a centre from which they are seen as one, as indeed they truly are. Thus will you give a new meaning to life. Above all things else this is the need of your race.

You have lost the sense of unity; you are conquered by the delusion of diversity; you are enslaved by the apparent separateness of things. So you have lost the meaning and the true vision of life. That vision must be recovered before any advance can be achieved. The keynote of the true vision of the meaning of life is unity in diversity; therefore, you must also teach unity.

Unity is the most intangible of all the attributes. Seek to grasp it in the lower world and it will evade you; therefore, you must rise above diversity, beyond form, past ideas, even leaving the land of joy behind you since joy is an idea. When the last vestige of an idea has been emptied from your soul, unity can be found.

XI

UNITY

A S there is a land of joy, so also there is a world where diversity is not, where there is unity alone. It is higher than the land of joy, for joy is the land of universal ideas, and unity is behind ideas. You cannot speak with any truth about this land, for words are diversities. Therefore may that land be named by one word alone; it is the land of unity. Not only is there no need for other words, there are no other words, for the one word "unity" expresses the whole. To analyse is to lose it; to synthesise is to lose it; unity cannot be analysed or synthesised; it is one.

What use, then, in the lower worlds? This—that you should obtain the *flavour* of it. The flavour of unity can be tasted by the mind, can even be expressed in action as *mutual endeavour*. Wherever there is mutual endeavour in the lower worlds, there men have caught the flavour of unity. In the higher worlds, above the mind, nought else exists, for they are closer to the world of unity; unity is their very life. Of it, perhaps, one sentence may be truly said; it is the embodiment of the will of God. Of that resistless will, no man living in the lower worlds may know. That it brought all things forth, that it holds all things in existence, that it is the driving power behind all life—these may be known; but they are its attributes and not the will itself; by will a man must rise through thought, through the land of ideas, even through unity, to the very Self. Then he may know the will of God.

This is a road which every man may take immediately, a road which one day every man will take irrevocably. If he would shorten his sojourn in the worlds of form, if his soul is satiated of form and separateness, then let him return: let him set forth upon the road by which he came, the ancient road, the well-worn road, the road which so many of his race and ours have trodden. This road is at his feet; let him set them thereon. It passes through his heart; he must pay toll with his heart's blood. It leads through his mind; he must be ready to lay aside his mind. Then he will find the bridge, the bridge so difficult to cross, for the way is very narrow here, but every step he takes widens it.

Upon the approaches to the bridge the human

race is standing today. The next stage in the evolution of the human mind will lead to the crossing of the bridge; it leads from the concrete to the abstract, from thought to idea, from separateness to union, from form to formlessness, from the impermanent to the permanent, from the mortal to the immortal, from the illusory to the actual, from the temporal to the eternal, from that which dies to that which is undying, from the natural man to the spiritual man, from the Not-Self to the Self. It is the bridge which all saints have crossed; it is the dividing line between spirit and mind. It is not a place, it is a state; it is not external, it is within.

After the bridge has been crossed, places disappear; only states of consciousness remain. He who would cross must leave himself behind; first, because no separated self can enter the state of union with the One; second, because the self must remain in lower worlds, as messenger and ambassador between the two lands on either side of the bridge. Having paid toll with the blood of the heart, having made ready to lay his mind aside, let the brave pilgrim step boldly on to the bridge; immediately he will find himself on the further side.

The bridge will not bear him standing; only as he moves across it may he make use of its support. Having crossed, he finds himself in the land of joy, where pain is for ever left behind, where parting is unknown, where knowledge dwells. He has reached the first resting place. Here he will find peace; here he will renew his courage and his strength, for the succeeding stages of his pilgrimage; here he will survey the road along which he has passed; here past and present will become one; here he may estimate the future and collect the many streams of energy that he has liberated in the past, and bind them into one. He will now begin to direct this single stream of power; he will float no longer upon its waves, at the mercy of the current, henceforth he will take control of himself. Knowing the past, he will possess the future. Here he will gather together the products of his many lives, and will assess their value; here, he will balance causation and effect; here, he begins to be the ruler of them both, knowing them as one; here, he sums up into a whole the zodiacal experiences of his many lives.

Thus, having crossed the bridge, will he live, thus will he labour, knowing his lower self (the man that he has left behind in worlds of form below the bridge) as his instrument. As instrument, henceforth, he must employ the lower man; upon mind, feeling and body he must play at will, render them silent at will, deprive them of all self-initiated volition, teach them to answer to his gentlest thought, develop to the full their automatism, so that they labour in the worlds of form as perfectly as if he himself employed them.

That portion of himself which he sent down, clothing it in form that it might command form, he now withdraws, leaving the form bereft of self, nought but an instrument. Later, he will withdraw still further; thus it is of very great importance that from the outset the form should be controlled, perfected, trained, ready to be laid aside at will, according to his need of freedom in the higher worlds, ready to be resumed and to serve with absolute efficiency. This is his duty in the world of form.

He will do his work with ease, because henceforth he works from above. No longer is a stream of thought or a rising feeling, or a craving of the flesh, associated with himself. He knows them as the not-self, repudiates their claims, and rules thought, feeling and flesh with his liberated will. They are but the brush with which he paints, in lower worlds, the vision which is his in worlds beyond the bridge. As pencil, he sharpens them, that he may draw truly the pattern he will weave upon the web of time and space, those illusory rulers of the worlds below.

These are the lessons he must learn ere once more he can take the road by which he shall attain liberation from the domain of time, space and form. He takes his bodies one by one, and perfects them, as a mechanic sharpens and adjusts his tools, that they may give him perfect service, never failing him in any task to which he sets his hand. The body must be made pure, light, responsive, accurate and controlled; it must be at ease. Through every nerve, sinew and muscle, through every organ, through flesh and skin and bone, there must be ease—perfect poise—utter restfulness. He must preserve his vital force as his most precious jewel in the lower world. Without it, the finest body will be useless; with it, all things may be done. It is the life force of the form through which he himself is immanent.

He will only use that portion of his body which

the immediate task demands; the remainder will be at rest, acting as a reservoir of vital force. Thus will he gain health, thus develop the special kind of strength which he will need in order to manifest, through the form which he maintains in worlds below, the vision and the power which he has won beyond the bridge. Thus will the pencil point be sharp, thus will he ensure against error, through failure, of the instrument.

This work will not be new, for, having glimpsed the vision of the land beyond the bridge for many lives before he crossed it, he has been preparing himself with such knowledge and power as he could command, while imprisoned in the lower worlds. His real, immortal self, with whom he is now united and identified, influenced him continually by brooding and suggestion, by atmosphere, by vision and by dream, so that he might prepare.

His feelings and thoughts he cultivates and refines, making them responsive only to the higher, eliminating all that which could respond to the lower. Having thus erected and perfected the downward pointing pyramid, he proceeds to the decoration and perfection of the higher, so that he may be ready for the next stage of the journey.

Thus, and thus alone, may lower man, in lower worlds, become regenerate. This is the meaning of the new birth. Man must die to his lower self in order that he may find new birth in the higher. As in earthly death, he finds rebirth into the worlds of feeling and of thought, so in this withdrawal of himself from the sovereignty of form, he may be said to die. He is not laid in any grave, nor does his body disappear before the eyes of men, yet he truly dies. This is the meaning of the crucifixion—the death, essential to birth. Every man must tread the road the Saviour trod.

There is a cyclic order in this birth and death. The crucifixion at the end of one cycle leads to birth at the commencement of the next. In never-ending spirals the great drama must be repeated, man ascending ever higher as he enacts that drama. It may well be called a crucifixion, for death upon the cross of material worlds must be repeated day by day, hour by hour, minute by minute, by him who would tread the Path.

Let no man think that he can hide behind a text, or take one step upon those spiral stairs by trusting in the sorrows of another, however great. It is this delusion which has delayed the progress of the Western world: that by the suffering of another, his sins, however he indulge, may be forgotten; that by bathing in another's blood he can find the feet of God. Such teachings may bring comfort to the mass, for behind them there is a truth, however much distorted; but he who would truly save the mass must leave the mass behind; relying on the strength of his inherent divinity alone, he must find and tread the path.

When the great resolve is once born within his heart, when once the first step has been taken, the help of many Saviours will be his, and with him They will freely share Their blood. This is the true Atonement, the at-one-ment which one day he must learn. They, the Liberated Men, the Great Ones of the earth; the perfected saints, the Holy Ones of God; the Guides and Masters of great hosts of angels; the Hidden Rulers of the world; the never-sleeping Watchers; They, Whose hands are never tired yet are ever full of labour for the world; Whose eyes are filled with pity, power and love, and infinite compassion—They stand, order upon order, living in realms beyond the land of peace and joy, resting in perfect unity with Him from Whom They sprang. They and Their angel hosts welcome the pilgrim; They send him strength, and cheer and comfort in his trials; They lend him angels to guide him on the Path. They smile upon his every fall, knowing that Their own achievements grew largely from their falls; They hide his eyes from the radiance of his own successes lest pride should rob him of humility. If from Their splendid heights, it were possible that They could feel a touch of fear, that fear would be for him who, essaying the path, has not yet died to pride.

Aided by the light from These, his great forerunners, having cast off ignorance and the superstition of the mass, strong in the strength of his divinity, the pilgrim climbs the hill, learning continually to die, voluntarily crucifying himself in worlds of form, that he may be born in formless worlds. He mortifies his flesh, but not in hermit's cave nor monkish cell, not by the scourge or shirt of hair, not by penances that destroy the fair beauty of the flesh; he mortifies himself by mind and will; his asceticism is of self-restraint in everything; his penance is the sacrifice of everything which would hinder his progress on the path; yet he knows no torture, and seldom, in his early days, anguish of soul.

Though thus he dies continually, and suffers all the pangs of death, he is not miserable. He is filled with joy, for he knows that every pang he feels, that every nail or spear that pierces him, liberates more power. As, from his wounds, his blood flows down upon the world below, more blood flows in.

Thus he learns to know the mystery of the wounded hands and feet and side. He knows that only when his hands are pierced with nails can he reach out and save the world; that only when his body is bowed beneath the cross can he bear its weight, and tread its road; only when he wears the crown of thorns can the kingly power emanate from him; he knows that only when his side is pierced, only when the soldier's spear (symbolic of strife and separateness and pain) has opened his heart, can he pay toll that he may pass along the road; that having given of his life's blood, he draws ever nearer to the land of joy where strife and separateness and pain can touch him no more, and, in the very act of giving, he hears the echo of the angel's voices singing in that land. Through his darkness and his pain, there comes a gleam of light, as from a candle burning in the window of his spiritual home.

So, ever, as he dies, is crucified in the worlds of form, men marvel at his fortitude; that even while he suffers, he smiles; that even in the darkness of his agony, his eyes are bright. Men do not, cannot, know that he hears the music and sees the vision of the higher world, and that, by this music and joy, his woe is overcome. Though the path is called the path of woe, it also may be called the path of joy. This should be added: that the joy is greater than the woe, the peace greater than the strife, the growing power greater than the weariness of pain, the light greater than the darkness. The moon it is which sets, but already upon his face are the first gleams of the rising sun.

Thus have I tried to tell the story of immortal man, who voluntarily submitted to the imprisonment of form, the deadening weight of flesh, that he might learn to master form and flesh. Having endured imprisonment of flesh for many lives, through many centuries, he now seeks to harvest all his gains. To do this he must disentangle his immortal part from the mortality which it wore, he must change the habit of a thousand lives and free himself from form. The Saviour named him *Prodigal*.

So he treads the path, seeking ever to beautify, to cultivate and refine his vehicles, his instruments, that, after he has died to them and died to their control, and won his birth in other worlds, he may use and find in them a many-sided diamond, which he may render still more highly polished, whose many facets he may now perfect, that through its translucent beauty, the new glory which is his may shine forth for the helping of his fellow-men. Such is his attitude to body and to form; ever he regards them as matter to be perfected and beautified.

This is the picture of his inner and his outer growth. Within he treads the path, finds the bridge that leads him from the mind, crosses it, and is identified with that of which he is a fragment and knows himself as an incarnated part, a separated gleam of light, from worlds of light, illuminating a portion of the world below. That part has now become the whole, that beam has been withdrawn into the parent light. The outer labour of the pilgrim on the path consists of polishing the matter which he has worn since, as a separated part, he came forth, of imparting to it a perfect translucency.

This is the meaning of spiritual death and spiritual birth. It is not a death as man would reckon death, for the form remains, apparently it lives and breathes. Symbolically, he truly dies, for he withdraws himself from form. Between the death which men call death and the death symbolical, there is this difference: that in the death of mortal flesh, the flesh disintegrates, while in the death symbolical, it is still preserved. This death refers more to the power of the form, and its control of life; so that he truly dies. In mortal death there is a moment when men can say "he lives," a moment when men say "he dies," a moment when men say "he is dead." But in the death of him who is reborn, death is continuous. This is a mystery which only he who treads the path can solve. If you would understand it, seek the road.

XII
THE PATH

WHAT reasons may be given to him who asks: "Why should I tread the Path of Woe?" There is but one reason, but it is all-sufficient—for love's sake. For it is love which brings about the first murmurings of discontent within the heart of man.

The value of his pilgrimage, the estimation of its worth, these may be calculated in terms of power to love. There comes a time in the long series of his many lives, when love demands an answer and assumes control, when man surrenders to the power of love. Love floods his being, fills his heart, finds an entrance into every nook and cranny of his soul. In him love's self becomes incarnate. Therefore, he can no longer deny love. Thus, filled with love, he

looks upon the world with its eyes, sees the whole
of manifested life in no other terms. Being himself
filled with love, he sees in all things an expression
of love. Love is his cosmos, love is his Self. Thus illumined, thus suffused, he sees the sorrows and suffering of the world, he hears the cry of every soul in
pain, the tears of sorrow fall upon his heart and
burn like drops of liquid flame.

The birds, the beasts, the fishes of the sea, find
entrance to his heart; he feels their anguish as they
die, slaughtered, butchered by those who know not
love. Seeing all this, feeling it deep within his soul,
he rises up to save, and finds that he is powerless,
that he cannot stay the hand of cruelty, he cannot
heal the gaping wound. He has neither the knowledge nor the power to take away the agonies of animals and men which tear his heart. Then conscious
of his impotence, so great is the anguish of his soul,
that the resolve that he will achieve both knowledge
and power is born.

Thus it is he finds and sets his feet upon the path.
If he ever should falter, love drives him on; if, in
his weakness, he turns back, love bars the way; if
he would stray down the pleasant by-ways of self-
delusion and self-indulgence, love turns him back.
If, with dead arguments and lifeless theories, phi-
losophers bid him stay, if they would close his ears
to cries of pain, love sounds her mighty trumpet
driving away harsh theories and philosophies,
burns within him so fiercely that he can rest no
more. If ever, while he walks, he deludes himself

with dreams, love awakens his soul, shatters his dreams; demands action. Should he stumble, love sustains him; at every milestone love smiles on him, taking stronger hold upon his heart.

Early upon the path, he finds that in the near approach of love are knowledge and power. He stretches forth his hand to help and sees the wound heal. Filled with a new joy, the joy of love expressed, he journeys on. Should one ask of him the reason of his pain, the reason is revealed by love. Thus knowledge grows, the knowledge of the cause of human woe. Then it is he hears love speak: "Knowledge and power must be wedded within you ere you can heal the sorrows of the world."

Thus love puts into his hands the standard he must bear, and writes the name of God upon it. Men see him as he passes on his way, they see the standard in his hand, but striving to read the Name, they see only power, knowledge, love. They cannot read the Name of God; they only see the armour, the sword and the shield which God lends to His son who journeys home.

Thus armed and equipped he crosses the bridge; hears the angels' welcoming songs; finds the source of knowledge, power and love; drinks his fill of these and, being filled, knows himself divine. God-like in his knowledge, power and love, he turns to heal and save the world which he has left behind. There is no pain which does not answer to the magic of his touch, no thirst that cannot be assuaged by his power, no evil that his knowledge cannot dissipate, no form of life, however high or low, in which he cannot see himself. He heals by identification. He drives away pain because he is pain's self, because pain is but the darker side of joy; being joy, he also is pain.

By leaving the world of men, he becomes their redeemer. This is his prize; this the goal; for this he started out upon the path. In the act of redeeming, he knows the greatest of all joys—the joy of love completely expressed.

You who read, have you not felt within your hearts the sorrows of the world? Have its cries of woe hurt your heart, or do you still sleep? You may sleep for a while, but the time will come when love will take you by the hand and set your feet upon the path. It is because of this that I have come, speaking in the name of your angel self, seeking to show you the road, to tell you of its splendour, of the glories yet to be revealed. Your own soul will awaken you to knowledge of your own divinity, you will arise and make of your earthly self a temple which shall be a worthy dwelling-place for your other self, the Self which is divine. The shrine of that temple must be within your heart; within that shrine, the Christ in you must come to dwell. For this reason, see to it that the temple of your body, the vehicle of your life, be beautiful, that through its beauty the splendour of the God within may be revealed.

XIII
METHODS *of* INVOCATION

THE ceremonies consist of a morning invocation to the Angels and an evening service of thanksgiving.

For this purpose the following suggestions are made: A shrine, in or out of doors, should be set apart and, where possible, used exclusively for this purpose; it should be consecrated by an appropriate ceremonial, which would have as its object the invocation of the power of the angels and the establishment of a centre and atmosphere in which contact and co-operation would be possible. The initial ceremony could be performed by a priest of the religion of the country, who is sympathetic to the ideals expressed, or by an occultist possessing the necessary knowledge and power.

In the east, should be an altar upon which worshippers should place (*a*) fragrant flowers, gathered freshly each day, (*b*) religious symbols, (*c*) a picture or statue of the Founder of the religion, (*d*) holy water, (*e*) incense, and (*f*) candles. The minimum —where other things are unobtainable—would be flowers and a single object of beauty.

Essential conditions are complete cleanliness, an atmosphere of utter purity, and a single desire for mutual co-operation of angels and men for the helping of the world.

Joy, simplicity and beauty should characterise all the ceremonies, preparations and arrangements.

All participants in the ceremonies should be clothed in simple robes of colour corresponding to that of the group of angels whose aid is being invoked; all undergarments should be white. One of the participants should officiate and act as link between the two corresponding groups of angels and men.

GROUPS OF ANGELS	COLOURS TO BE WORN
Guardian angels of the home	Rose and soft green
Healing angels	Deep sapphire blue
Angels of maternity and birth	Sky blue
Ceremonial angels	White
Angels of music	White
Nature angels	Apple-green
Angels of Beauty and Art	Yellow (the wisdom colour)

Prayers may be offered for particular purposes. Where more than one group of angels is invoked, the officiant for each should be robed in the appropriate colour and perform the appropriate ceremony.

Procedure: Once begun the services should be maintained regularly and are best performed immediately after the morning and evening ablutions. The presence of children—who should wear white —is desirable.

All should enter in procession, the children leading, the officiants last. The children should sit in a half-circle, facing the altar, in front of the elders, leaving a passage in the centre for the officiants.

Where very young, aged, sick people or pregnant women are present, they should be placed nearest the altar, the rest, with the exception of children, standing in straight rows behind them.

Each officiant, one for each group of angels, will advance to the altar in turn, repeat the appropriate invocation, during which he will lift the bowl of flowers above his head, following them with his eyes. When taking his special part in the ceremony, the officiant should use all his powers of thought and will to summon the angels. (The measure of effectiveness in all ceremony is proportionate to the amount of knowledge, will and thought-power employed by the officiant.)

All present will join with him, to the utmost of their capacity, following intently the meaning of the prayer.

No undue physical strain should be produced by the effort made, but ceremonies should not be allowed to degenerate into mere repetition of formulae. At the same time, an intense feeling of joy in, and a sense of anticipation of, the companionship of the angels must be steadily maintained.

* * * * * * *

At the evening service of thanksgiving, after the prayer, let the officiant hold up the bowl of flowers, offering their beauty and their sweetness to the angels, and pouring through them deep love and gratitude from his heart towards the angel hosts. Let all present similarly pour out their love through the officiant and the flowers; then sit in silence, giving thanks and making their private prayers; then go directly to bed.

When it is not possible for the young, the sick, the aged or the pregnant to be present, the group or a part of the group should go straight to their rooms from the shrine, bearing a second bowl of flowers, which has been standing on the altar during the ceremony. Then, facing the patient, the particular ceremony required should be repeated—invoking angel guardians for the young and aged, building angels for the pregnant, healing angels for the sick. Where only one room is thus visited, the bowl of flowers should be left on a small shrine in the room; where a number of visits are called for, the flowers should be distributed among the rooms, placed in vases on the respective shrines. Where an appropriate object of beauty cannot be procured for these shrines, flowers will suffice.

* * * * * * *

At risk of repetition it should be made clear that this conception must be preserved in its simplest possible form, entirely free from all sensationalism or elaborate ceremonial; nor should any attempt be made to obtain close personal contact with individual angels, or to employ them from motives of personal gain, interest or curiosity. Such endeavours would almost invariably lead to disaster, and must be rigorously avoided. It should be as natural to work with angels as with human beings, or as with domestic animals; and qualities of SIMPLICITY, PURITY, DIRECTNESS and IMPERSONALITY must characterise all who would successfully take part in such endeavours.

A knowledge and appreciation of the teachings of the Ancient Wisdom should make depression and similar moods impossible. Complete confidence in the Divine power and Divine justice characterise the angel hosts, and if men would work with them they, too, must attain those qualities. The ability to judge the importance of a temporary circumstance by seeing its relation to the whole, to the completed scheme, must be developed, so that it becomes impossible to be unduly elated, cast down, or overcome by any particular event or succession of events. The power to work on, with utter faith, with complete certainty, in spite of the apparent failure of any particular endeavour, must be sought; for thus the angels work. Christians would do well to remember and repeat frequently the Collect for the day of St. Michael and All Angels.

*   *   *   *   *   *   *

Let me picture to you what may still come, give you a vision of that which lies ahead.

Picture a vast plain, in a far clime, under a clear sky, where thousands and thousands of your people gather—and, with them, the sick, the aged, the young—and form, in great figures on the plain, stars, triangles, pentagons, invoking us, until, descending to your earth, we come, visible, as robed in flesh—a glorious descent into your midst. Not we alone, but with us members of your race, coming from the ranks of Those to whom earth can teach no more. There we come among the multitude, to heal, to guide and to inspire, and, ere we depart, with promise of early return, to pray with them, uplifting all to the feet of Him Who is the Father of us all, our Logos and our Lord. In every land, to every people, thus might we come.

XIV
INVOCATIONS *and* PRAYERS

Morning Invocations

DEVAS OF CEREMONY

HAIL, brethren of the devic hosts!
Come to our aid.
Give us your fiery devic power
As we give you our human love.

Fill every place with power and life!
Share with us the labours of this earth,
That the life-force within be set free.

MUSIC

HAIL, devas of Music!
Come to our aid.
Sing to us your songs of joy;
Fill us with divine harmony.
Awaken us, that we may hear your voice;
Attune our ears to your song;
Ensoul our earthly music with your light.
Share with us the labours of the earth,
That men may hear the melodies you sing.
Beyond the realms of Space and Time.

GUARDIAN DEVAS OF THE HOME

HAIL, Guardian Angels of the Home!
Come to our aid,
Share with us our work and play.
Be with us that we may hear your wings.
And feel your breathe upon our cheek;
Come close, and sense our human love.

Take our hands in yours,
Lift us for a while
From the burden of this flesh.

Grant us to share with you
Your wondrous freedom throughout space
Your vivid life in sunlit air,
Your great intensity of joy,
Your unity with Life.

Help us so to work and play
That the time may be brought near
When all our race
Shall know you well,
And hail, you brother pilgrims
On the path to God.

Hail, Guardian Angels of the Home!
Come to our aid,
Share with us our work and play,
That the Life within may be set free.

BUILDING ANGELS

HAIL, devic hosts who build!
Come to our aid;
Help this new birth
Into the world of men.

Strengthen the mother in her pain;
And send your gracious angels
To attend the bed of birth,
And usher in the dawn
Of this new life.
Give to the coming child
The blessing of our Lord.

Hail, devic hosts who build!
Come to our aid;
Help this new birth into the world of men,
That the divinity within may be set free.

HEALING ANGELS

HAIL, devas of the Healing Art!
Come to our aid.
Pour forth your healing life
Into this . . . (place or person).

Let every cell be charged anew
With vital force.
To every nerve give peace.
Let tortured sense be soothed.
May the rising tide of life
Set every limb aglow,
As, by your healing power,
Both soul and body are restored.

Leave here (or there) an angel watcher,
To comfort and protect,
Till health returns or life departs,
That he may ward away all ill,
May hasten the returning strength—
Or lead to peace when life is done.

Hail, devas of the Healing Art!
Come to our aid,
And share with us the labours of this earth,
That God may be set free in man.

ANGELS OF NATURE

HAIL, devas of the earth and sky!
Come to our aid.
Give fertility to our fields,
Give life to all our seeds,
That this our earth may be fruitful.

Hail, devas of the earth and sky!
Come to our aid;
Share with us the labours of our world
That the divinity within may be set free.

ANGELS OF BEAUTY AND OF ART

HAIL, angels of the Hand of God!
Come to our aid.
Impress upon our worlds
Of thought, of feeling and of flesh,
A sense of Divine Beauty.
Help us to see the vision of the Self,
To recognise in all created things
The Beauty of the Self;
That through the Beauty we may find,
Hid deep behind external veils
Of colour, line and form,
The Very Self,
Thus, having helped us,
Inspire us with the power
To give expression in our lives
To all that we have seen—
To the Good, the True, the Beautiful.

Grant that we may see and know
You, the angels of His Hand,
That, seeing, we may learn to share
Your task of shedding beauty on the world.

Hail, angels of the Hand of God!
Come to our aid.
Share with us the labours of this earth,
That the beauty within may be revealed.

Evening Hymns of Prayer and Thanksgiving

MAY blessings from above
Flow forth and beautify the human love
Which we in gratitude pour forth
To you, our angel helpers of this day.
Accept our love and grateful prayers
And help us, so to live and work,
That ever, day by day,
Your hosts shall find us growing
Akin to you.

We crave this night your guardianship for all,
Be with the young, the aged, and the sick;
Surround their beds with wings of light and peace,
Cherish them, we pray, until the dawn.
And, as the sun once more returns
To give us life and warmth and light,
Let us again prelude our work
With salutation and with praise
To Him Who is the Father of us all;
That, hand in hand and side by side,
His human and His angel sons
May labour in His Name
To bring about the glorious day
When, in our world and theirs,
His Will alone shall reign.

                                        AMEN

NIGHT gathers to its close our earthly day,
And now we gather here, our angel guest,
To offer thee our love and gratitude;
To thank thee for thy service.

May Those Who labour ever night and day,
Pour down upon thee blessings manifold,
Send thee Their super-human love and grace;
May Their compassion fill thee, and Their life,
Till, overflowing, streams of love shall fall
From Thee to us, flow back from us to thee,
Binding our hearts in bonds of brotherhood,
Uniting us by links of love divine.
We pray thee, ever answer our call,
For we would ever open our hearts to thee.
Come closer, blessed messengers of God,
We would hear Him in the beating of thy wings.

In silence, in serenity of heart and mind,
We greet thee, at the closing of this day;
May He enfold thee in His everlasting arms
Till His radiance and His joy shine through thee.

Be with the children, blessed one, this night;
Be with the aged and the sick;
By each bed a guardian angel stand
That all may sleep in peace, waking betimes
To feel thy guardian presence with them still.

AMEN